D1030411

ICE HOCKEY LEGENDS

Martin Brodeur

Sergei Fedorov

Peter Forsberg

Wayne Gretzky

Dominik Hasek

Brett Hull

Jaromir Jagr

Paul Kariya

John LeClair

Mario Lemieux

Eric Lindros

Mark Messier

CHELSEA HOUSE PUBLISHERS

ICE HOCKEY LEGENDS

MARIO LEMIEUX

Brian Tarcy

CHELSEA HOUSE PUBLISHERS
Philadelphia

Produced by Daniel Bial and Associates
New York, New York

Picture research by Alan Gottlieb
Cover illustration by Earl Parker

3 5 7 9 8 6 4 2

Library of Congress Cataloging-in-Publication Data

Tarcy, Brian.
    Mario Lemieux / by Brian Tarcy.
       p. cm. — (Ice hockey legends)
    Includes bibliographical references and index.
    Summary: Hailing from Montreal, Canada, Lemieux is the star of the
Pittsburgh Penguins hockey team, known for his scoring prowess and
stickhandling skill.
    ISBN 0-7910-4558-7
    1. Lemieux, Mario, 1965- —Juvenile literature. 2. Hockey players—
Canada—Biography—Juvenile literature. 3. Hodgkin's disease—Patients—
Canada—Biography—Juvenile literature. 4. Pittsburgh Penguins (Hockey
team)—Juvenile literature. [1. Lemieux, Mario, 1965- . 2. Hockey players.]
I. Title. II. Series.
GV848.5.L46T37 1997
796.962'092—dc21   97-27365
                                                        CIP
                                                         AC

CONTENTS

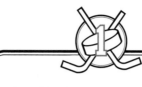

A MOMENT IN TIME

There is a pass and Mario Lemieux has the puck. It is May 17, 1991, in Pittsburgh's Civic Arena. This is not just any game. It's the Stanley Cup finals—hockey's equivalent of football's Super Bowl or baseball's World Series. The winners will hold aloft an actual cup and consider themselves the world champions of professional hockey this year.

It is the second game of the best-of-seven series, late in the second period. (Hockey games are scheduled to have three periods, but ties produce overtime periods—particularly in the playoffs when no game can end in a tie.) The score is the Pittsburgh Penguins 2, Minnesota North Stars 1, but the North Stars, who won the first game of the series, have had recent momentum in this game. They scored earlier this quarter. They've been dominating the puck, controlling it much more than Pittsburgh. If the North Stars

Goalie Jon Casey watches carefully as Mario Lemieux whizzes behind the net during the 1991 Stanley Cup finals.

Casey sprawls one way but Lemieux has changed direction on him—and the puck is in for the deciding goal.

can come back in this game, they will take a commanding lead in the series—perhaps too much for Pittsburgh to overcome.

If the underdog North Stars could somehow go on to win this series, the reputation of Mario Lemieux as a big-time player would suffer a terrible blow. Already in his short career, Lemieux has been questioned. No one has questioned his ability—he has put up astronomical numbers. There have been questions about his heart, his desire.

Part of it is simply Lemieux. He is a quiet man. He is not a flashy modern-type player who declares his greatness to the world. He doesn't thump his chest. Instead, he silently goes about his business of finding the net with the puck.

In his career, he has been phenomenal. Still, he hasn't won anything. If the North Stars come back here and take a 2-0 lead in the series, the whispers about his lack of desire will grow louder.

Lemieux is deep in his own end. The stretch of ice lays before him and he eyes it like a predator eyes a field between himself and his prey. He appears at first glance to be moving at a casual pace. But he is already skating faster than everybody else. Speed is his game.

He attacks the defense, which is braced yet aware of the size difference. Lemieux is 6' 4", large by hockey standards. He does not intimidate with words. He is bigger than most hockey players, and he carries himself like he knows it. Power is his game.

The defense also understands that Lemieux can do almost anything with the puck. Well, they think they understand. But they haven't seen what he is about to do to them. They haven't seen this particular brand of magic. He is about to pull a new trick from up his sleeve. You see, finesse is his game.

The thing about Lemieux is that his game is complete—more complete than any hockey player who has ever donned skates. He has that perfect combination of speed, power, and finesse that makes him a living legend.

In every great athlete's career, there are defining moments. As Lemieux approaches the two defensemen, this becomes just such a moment.

With his lethal combination of speed, power, and finesse, some have said that he is the greatest player in the game. Others scoff and say he has never won a championship. They point to Wayne Gretzky, often considered the greatest hockey player ever, who can claim four Stanley

Cup championships as evidence of his greatness.

For many people, Gretzky is the Babe Ruth of hockey. He is considered not just a once-in-a-generation player. He is thought to be more than even a once-in-a-lifetime player. Gretzky's nickname is "The Great One." For most of his career, experts predicted that those alive now would never see anyone challenge Gretzky's reputation as the greatest ever. Here was Lemieux, doing just that—and while Gretzky was still far from retired.

Nearly a quarter century of bad hockey by men in Penguins uniforms seems to follow Lemieux down the ice. He plays for what was for years an inept franchise.

Lemieux was the number one pick in the 1984 draft and was heralded as the savior when he arrived. The team was rumored to be moving. Financial problems were the biggest news from team headquarters. It was a team without life.

Then the Montreal native arrived in Pittsburgh with a flair, scoring in his first period in a Penguins uniform. He scored and scored, yet he stayed home in the spring. For six long years the savior didn't win championships. He won scoring titles. Scoring titles don't make you the greatest in the game. He knew that. So did everybody else—especially Gretzky's fans.

Then a wonderful thing started happening to Lemieux. The Penguins began to surround him with good players.

Still, there had been whispers over the years that Lemieux didn't always try his hardest or that sometimes he took a dive. In other words, some felt that he often fell on purpose when he was hit to draw a penalty. There was talk that he was a "floater" who wouldn't always defend his position. There was talk that he had never won anything. They said he lacked the will to win.

In the semifinals, the Penguins seemed to prove the whisperers wrong, sweeping the vaunted Boston Bruins. Now the Penguins are down one game to none, and the North Stars appear to be rallying in this game.

Lemieux has the puck. He takes an outlet pass from Phil Borque, and he moves up the ice in that classic Lemieux overdrive. It's such a smooth shift that the average fan might not realize how fast he is going.

The two defensemen realize it. After all, they are professionals. Still, there's little they can do about it except try to skate back to their zone as fast as possible to try to impede his way to the goal.

Already, in this game, Lemieux made a perfect pass across the slot to Kevin Stevens for a power play goal. (A power play is a period of time when one team has to play with fewer players because someone on that team committed a penalty and must sit out. The team with more players on the ice than the others is in a power play.) Two of Lemieux's breakaways in the game led to power plays because the North Stars had dragged him down. He had also slammed North Star Mike Modano into the glass with a legal check. He had already shown considerable will to win.

Once, early in his career, Lemieux addressed the criticism. "Maybe it's because I'm tall, I don't know," he said. "People say I'm not so fast, but I know I can skate with these guys in this league. I like to play deep in the offensive zone, so I'm always one of the last back on defense. But that's how I score goals."

Now, with the puck in his hands, he can actually do something to increase the slim one-goal lead. He charges toward defenseman Shawn Chambers, and he remembers earlier in the game trying to get outside Chambers and not succeeding. Chambers caught up with him that time.

This time, Lemieux dips his shoulder. He jukes outside. He cuts back, and with his backhand he sends the puck between Chambers's legs. Chambers is left standing there, guarding air. Lemieux catches up with the puck and has no one to beat except Minnesota goaltender Jon Casey. It's a split-second war of nerves. Each tries to read the other. Casey is good. But Lemieux is in another stratosphere.

Casey waits.

Lemieux puts the puck on his forehand, ready to shoot.

Casey bites, moving to his left to cut off Lemieux's angle.

Lemieux is prepared for Casey's actions. He falls to his knees at an incredible speed and switches the puck over to his backhand.

Suddenly, Casey has no angle. All he has is the right side of his net totally unprotected.

It's almost invisible, how fast Lemieux does it. Swoosh. The puck goes right in the empty net.

Bang! Lemieux's forward motion slams him into the goal post.

It is a moment frozen in time: the sleight of hand, the majesty of it, the pure speed and nerve of Lemieux changing the momentum of a Stanley Cup series. It is a play for the ages.

More importantly, Minnesota's control of the game is gone. The score is 3-1. The arena full of

Penguin fans becomes a collective soul. There is only joy. Lemieux has done it again.

The North Stars are in shock. They had shut down other prolific scorers on the way here. Earlier in the playoffs, they kept the St. Louis Blues' Brett Hull under control. But Lemieux just acted like a bold surgeon, cutting through the defense.

The game ends with the North Stars losing by a score of 4-1. A Minnesota assistant coach, Chris Resch, gave the *New York Times* his assessment of Lemieux. "The problem is, he is the best on breakaways. You'd like to challenge him, you'd like to wait on him, but whatever you seem to do, he can counter. So you just hope that he gets pressured or that the puck bounces and he loses the puck," said Resch.

The only way to stop Lemieux, clearly, is to hope.

In Game 2, Lemieux destroyed the North Stars' hope. He showed that his will to win was as big as his enormous talent. He had overcome great obstacles. Never again, his fans might have thought, would he have to face so much adversity.

They couldn't have imagined what lay in store.

GROWING UP IN MONTREAL

When Mario Lemieux was nine years old, his father, Jean-Guy Lemieux, was already convinced that his son was on his way to the National Hockey League (NHL). Mario's father recalled it this way for the *New York Times*: "He was playing mite hockey then, with boys who were nine and 10 years old, and he was already the leader of the team. In every category, scoring and size, he was always bigger."

Lemieux was born on October 5, 1965. Mario's father was a construction worker. His mother was a homemaker, taking care of Mario and his two older brothers, Alain and Richard.

The Lemieux family lived in Montreal, Canada, the second-largest city in that country. Montreal is also the largest city in the province of Quebec. Like most people in Quebec, the Lemieux are "French-Canadian," which means that Mario grew up speaking French, not English.

Mario Lemieux accepts the most valuable player award after a tournament in Sorel, Canada. He was six years old at the time.

Canadian children happily play baseball, basketball, and football (although the Canadian Football League uses rules slightly different from the United States's National Football League); however, hockey is the most popular sport in Canada. It has only been in the past ten years that Americans have started to hold their own against the best Canadian stars.

Boys in Montreal grow up dreaming of playing in the NHL, and specifically for the Montreal Canadiens. The Canadiens are the most storied franchise in the NHL, much like the New York Yankees in baseball or the Boston Celtics in basketball. The team has won more championships than any other in the NHL. They have been dominant.

All three Lemieux boys played hockey. Richard, the oldest, gave up the sport fairly early, but Alain was a good player, At age 18, he joined the Laval Voisons of the Canadian Junior Hockey League.

Mario began playing hockey when he was young on an outdoor rink not far from home. The rink, in fact, was just a frozen pond behind his Roman Catholic parish church, St. Jean de Matha. If it snowed—and in Montreal it often snowed—the boys would spend hours shoveling the snow off the ice so they could play.

Lemieux and his friends would play for hours every night, often continuing to skate well after sundown. "I never missed an opportunity to play if I had a chance," he later recalled.

Mario's brothers also loved to play hockey, but it was clear from an early age that Mario was the most skilled. When Mario was 16, he was already showing an ability to play with, and, in fact, outplay, older boys. He joined the same team his

At age nine, Mario (far right) poses with his teammates after they won the 1974 Tom Thumb hockey tournament.

brother had played with, the Laval Voisons. There, he began to establish a reputation that spread far beyond Montreal.

By this age, he had already reached his full height of 6'4" and weighed 200 pounds. Most kids his age would find it hard to maneuver such a large body that had come on relatively quickly. Not Mario. That first year, he was a wizard on the ice, scoring 30 goals to go along with 66 assists for a total of 96 points. (An assist is a pass that is converted by another player into a goal.) The following year he did much better. He scored 84 goals, and added 100 assists for a total of 184 points.

Beyond his scoring prowess, he was an incredible stickhandler. He could do things with the puck that seemed like magic.

Then there was his size.

Hockey had normally been a game of average-sized men. Although some had come along who were big like Lemieux, no one had ever seen such a big man with such skills. NHL scouts flocked to the rink to see if what they heard was true.

In his final year at Laval, Lemieux put up numbers that seemed to fly into the stratosphere. He had 133 goals and 149 assists for a total of 282 points.

All the while, he and his team went on incredible road trips for games. Sometimes the team would travel five hours by bus, play the game, and then travel five hours home. Some mornings after those long road trips, he had to head right to school.

It never bothered him. He just kept scoring. Jack Button, the Washington Capitals' director of player personnel, said, "If he really wanted to, he might have doubled his point production with Laval."

Needless to say, Lemieux won every award the league offered. As his reputation grew, so did the intensity of the opposition. He often found that he had a "shadow," a player on the other team who spent his whole time following Lemieux, hoping to make it difficult for him to score. In one game, while he was playing for Laval, Lemieux's "shadow" was being particularly brutal. He was slashing and hooking. It also seemed as if he were trying to hurt Lemieux.

Finally, the quiet Lemieux had had enough. He dropped his gloves and turned to the other player. In one punch, the other player was down.

Lemieux received a major penalty, but the other player got the message and never played dirty against Lemieux again.

He also showed a willingness to stand up to those older than him. Once, his coach at Laval berated him for getting four penalties in a game. Lemieux didn't like being yelled at, so he yelled back. "What about the seven points I scored?" he said.

The coach agreed that Lemieux had played well.

While NHL scouts were enamored with Lemieux, there was already a superstar in the league who was rewriting all the record books. His name was Wayne Gretzky.

Gretzky, although not the size of Lemieux, was a wizard on the ice. While Lemieux was scoring at a prolific pace in the Canadian Major Junior Hockey League, Gretzky was already doing it where it really counts—in the National Hockey League.

People said that Gretzky was the Babe Ruth of hockey. People said there would never be another Gretzky. But then, when people began to see Lemieux play, they began to think that maybe, just maybe, somebody could challenge Gretzky's preeminence.

THE EARLY YEARS

In Pittsburgh, while Lemieux was doing astonishing things for Laval, the Penguins were having a horrible season.

The NHL draft is set up to give the top pick to the worst team. The Penguins were the worst team.

There were rumors that Lemieux would refuse to play for a weak NHL team. Lemieux said the rumors were not true. His only concern, he said, was to get to the NHL as fast as possible and not spend time in the minors. "I'd like to get to a team that is very low and get that team up in a few years," he said.

Indeed, while still with Laval, Lemieux once commented on how much the Penguins needed a guy like him. "I saw their last game at the Montreal Forum," he told *Hockey News* in February 1984. "They have trouble scoring goals. I score goals and set up my wingers."

At age 20, Lemieux signed a contract that made him the second-highest-paid player in hockey. Only Wayne Gretzky was earning more.

In his first shift in his first pro game, Mario scored a goal.

The Penguins were so bad that they were teetering on the edge of nonexistence. There were rumors of bankruptcy. The owner wanted to sell. Attendance was down.

"I knew of the Pittsburgh situation," said Lemieux. "The team had been waiting for someone to come in and take charge. I was ready for that challenge."

Penguin General Manager Eddie Johnston knew that he wanted to pick Lemieux, and so Lemieux was drafted by the Penguins.

Lemieux at first did not want to play for Pittsburgh. In fact, at the draft, he shunned the long tradition of each top NHL draft pick posing with a jersey of the team that picked him. Being a French-speaking native of Montreal, Lemieux wanted to play in Canada, or at least for a more successful franchise.

In the NHL, players don't have a choice of where to play. Eventually, Lemieux realized that, and he came to accept his future as a Penguin. He signed with the Penguins for $350,000 a year for two seasons.

When he signed, the *Pittsburgh Post-Gazette* described the press conference this way: "He stood there, finally, with a Penguin on his chest, smiling, saying all the right things, trying very hard to look like a messiah."

Lemieux was anointed when he arrived in Pittsburgh. The press conference featured many glowing tributes to the new star, but Mario downplayed them. "I try not to think about what they said," he explained. "I just want to go on the ice and do the best I can."

The first order of business was to pick a number. Something like this, seemingly minor, turned out to be quite symbolic. Lemieux picked 66, which is Gretzky's 99 turned upside down.

Part of the plan for the 18-year-old rookie was for him to live with a local Pittsburgh family while he established himself in the area. Pittsburgh general manager Eddie Johnston wanted Lemieux to live with a family to give him some stability. "Just to see that he gets milk at the dinner table," joked Johnston.

Lemieux was not worried about food, only hockey. He described his diet this way: "Hamburgers, french fries, pizza. Not junk food, fast food."

Another reason for placing Lemieux with a family was that he spoke almost no English. Being away from home at 18 years old was very difficult. Not speaking English in Pittsburgh was even more difficult. Living with a family made the transition easier.

When he was with Laval, he had taken a course in English, but his English was still not very good. In Pittsburgh, he found an interesting way to learn the language. He watched soap operas.

And he played hockey.

Boy, did he play. In his first shift during the first period of his first game, against the Boston Bruins, he scored a goal. He wasn't the first person to do that, but it's a very rare feat—even rarer than the number of baseball players who have hit home runs in their first at-bat.

He used his speed to get past people. He used his incredible vision to make passes that seemed impossible. He used his strength to set himself in the "slot," the area in front of the goal. Opposing players tried to push him out, but they couldn't. He was just too big.

He used his ability to see holes past the goalie to score. He was deft with the puck. He could seemingly do anything.

Paul Martha, the Penguins' vice president and general counsel, said that Lemieux's arrival was "the biggest thing that's ever happened to the Pittsburgh Penguin organization."

People in Pittsburgh loved it. In his rookie year, attendance jumped 46 percent from the previous year. To them, it was like discovering a different sport from the one they had been watching for years. This young man could play *hockey*.

Everybody in Pittsburgh wanted a piece of him. Before Lemieux's first home game in Pittsburgh, Penguins director of marketing Paul Steigerwald said, "We've been besieged with more requests for Lemieux. Of our advertisers, everyone wants him. He's appearing at Gimbels. He has five more appearances set up at various stores."

Lemieux likes goaltenders—but only if they're on his team. Here he helps out Penguin goalie Robert Romano in a game against the Rangers.

There were many promotions connected with Lemieux. The Penguins were quick to take advantage of his star attraction. At one game, the Penguins gave out life-size posters of Lemieux. It was a shrewd move, guaranteeing they would be hanging in bedrooms and dens across the Pittsburgh area as young people dreamed of following in their new star's footsteps.

Steigerwald knew how much Lemieux meant to the team. "We've had two last-place finishes in a row," he said. "Under normal circumstances, a team finishing last would lose [season ticket holders] significantly, but having the number one draft pick and getting Mario has made a big difference."

There was a problem, though. Often, it seemed like he was the only one on the team who could play. Although the other players were indeed professionals, they were not a good enough supporting cast to make up a winning team.

But Steigerwald, like many, saw something special. "He's a class kid all the way. He perfectly understands why he's here, what's expected from him, and the good he can do for our organization.

"He's so refreshing," he continued. "He's so cooperative, he hasn't asked for money, none of that 'me, me, me' stuff. A lot of the things he may say sound cliche-ish, but he's sincere. He shows leadership qualities. He has a great personality. Mario's larger than life. He can be a hero, he's got star quality. He's someone to look up to. And I believe he'll live up to it."

That first year, Lemieux was a force. He scored 43 goals and added 57 assists for a total of 100 points. No one was surprised when he was named NHL Rookie of the Year.

Still, the team finished with 24-51-5 record. Only one team in the league had a worse record. There was more work to be done. Meanwhile, Lemieux kept getting better.

In 1986, he was the most valuable player of the NHL All-Star game. He led his team to a 6-4 victory. "Winning the All-Star Game MVP really made him feel he belonged," said Eddie Johnston. "From then on, he took off."

He took advantage of his size in extraordinary ways. Instead of just pushing people around, he was actually able to use his size to keep people away from the puck, while at the same time handling the puck with unusual deftness.

He seemed to play games with defensemen. He would put the puck out for a defensemen to take it away, and then when the defensemen tried, he pulled it back in with his long arms and then used his speed and power to get past them.

That second season, he scored 48 goals and had 93 assists for 141 points. That year, Gretzky, on a much better team, scored 52 goals and had a record 163 assists for 215 points.

Lemieux was getting closer to Gretzky's prowess, but he wasn't there yet. He did win the Lester B. Pearson Award, which is given to the league's best player as selected by the Players' Association. It was the first time in four years that the award was not given to Gretzky. The Penguins were impressed enough to give Lemieux a new $2.75 million contract for five years.

Lemieux didn't seem fazed by the large amount of money. "I was really nervous when we were ready to sign the new contract," said Bob Perno, Lemieux's agent. "So was his dad. While we were sitting in the Penguins' offices, Mario said, 'Let's play Intellivision Football.' So we played and he was more interested in beating me in that game than he was in signing that huge contract."

In 1986, Lemieux was presented with the Dapper Dan Man of the Year Award, an honor given to Pittsburgh's finest. He was the first hockey player to win the award and the second-youngest winner ever. Lemieux, though gratified by receiving the award, said that his personal goal was merely to win. "That's all I want to do," he said. "Win and make the playoffs."

Neither happened that year. He missed 17 games due to injuries. Nevertheless, he finished with 54 goals and 53 assists for 107 points. But the Penguins again didn't make the playoffs.

B y 1987, despite being a prolific scorer, Lemieux had still not played in any big games. During his first four seasons, the Penguins did not make the playoffs.

He had begun to get a reputation, the kind of reputation that no player wants. People called him lazy. They said that he lacked motivation. He was at times sensational during the regular NHL seasons, but at other times he seemed to be on cruise control.

Then, in the summer of 1987, Lemieux teamed up with the man who was universally viewed as the best player ever to lace up a pair of skates—Wayne Gretzky. It was for the tournament called the Canada Cup, an international competition in which national teams from around the world competed.

Team Canada was indeed something special. Gretzky came to the tournament with his usual astonishing intensity. Teamed with Gretzky,

Lemieux got to play alongside Wayne Gretzky at the 1987 Canada Cup.

Lemieux seemed to learn a bit about what it takes to compete at the highest level of the sport. "Every shift, every time we were on the ice, Wayne tried to do the impossible," said Lemieux.

Lemieux learned from Gretzky. He learned the value of harder work. He learned about passion for hockey, a nonstop attitude of attacking the game as if it were the last game he would ever play. Soon people began to believe that maybe there were two masters. The Canada Cup, with its all-star-like cast of teams and the nationalistic fervor that goes with playing for one's country, was certainly the highest level.

Lemieux rose to the challenge. "He came forward more than any other player in the tourney, with leaps and bounds," John Muckler, an assistant coach with Canada, told the *Boston Globe.* "He accepted the challenge."

Indeed, he did. Lemieux scored a tournament-high 11 goals and led Canada to victory. The teaming of Lemieux and Gretzky was just the tonic Lemieux needed to push his career to the next level. "He was a different person when he came back from that," Pittsburgh forward Phil Borque told *Sports Illustrated.*

Lemieux said, "Playing alongside Wayne gave me a lot of confidence in myself. And I brought it back to Pittsburgh."

In 1988, Lemieux again was named to the All-Star game. Regulation time ended with the score tied at 5-5, and Lemieux had played a part in all of his team's goals. He had two goals and three assists—but he wasn't through yet. In the overtime, he scored on a quick wrist shot after giving a defender a fake that sent him reeling in the wrong direction. Naturally, Lemieux won the Most Valuable Player award.

That year, he won his first scoring title. He had 70 goals and 98 assists for 168 points. Gretzky came in second with 40 goals and 109 assists to finish 19 points back. There was a changing of the guard, even as Gretzky was still in his prime.

Gretzky had won the Hart Trophy, the NHL's most valuable player award, for eight seasons in a row. This year, it went to Lemieux.

Before the 1989 season, Lemieux signed a five-year, $10-million contract with the Penguins. Plus, there was an additional $3 million in bonuses. The Penguins knew the premier player deserved to be paid premier dollars.

For the next two seasons, Lemieux outscored the great Gretzky during the regular NHL season. In 1989, he scored 104 points—in the first 36 games. Only one player ever reached 100 points faster in a season—Wayne Gretzky.

Everyone was talking about Lemieux. "Once he gets behind you, he cannot be stopped," said his new coach, Gene Ubriaco.

In 1988, Lemieux won his first scoring title.

Even his teammates were awed. Randy Cunneyworth once saw Lemieux skate past and around the entire Vancouver Canucks team. "They were literally falling at his feet, one after another," he said. "I froze that picture: three guys behind Mario in a heap. He ended up behind the net and just reached around and stuffed the puck in. I was on the bench and I just started laughing."

That year, Lemieux led the Penguins to their first playoff appearance during his career. He ended the season with 85 goals and 114 assists for 199 points, which led the league. The team finished in second place in the Patrick Division.

Tom Barrasso was a key player in the Penguins' run for the Stanley Cup in 1992.

In their first playoff series, the Penguins' teamwork dominated the New York Rangers, and the Penguins won four straight games to sweep the series. In the division finals, the Penguins played the Philadelphia Flyers. When the series was tied at two games each, Lemieux took over. He had eight points in Game 5 to give the Penguins a 3-2 series lead, but the Flyers stormed back to win the next two games and end the Penguins' season.

The 1989-90 season was supposed to build on the Penguins' success. The only talk in Pittsburgh was of a Stanley Cup, but the season began poorly for the Penguins. They lost games they should have won—in fact, they lost more games than they were winning. Lemieux wasn't playing well at all.

Mario couldn't explain it. "I'm not skating as well as last year," he said. "I have no jump, no energy."

Lemieux and the Penguins had some successful games, but as the playoffs started to loom, the local newspapers broke the story that Mario had been playing all season with a herniated disk in his back. He tried a back brace, but he was in too much pain. He took himself out. With their leader in poor health, the Penguins finished in fifth place, out of the playoffs again.

In July 1990, Lemieux was forced to have surgery on his back. He hoped the operation would bring him back to where he was before, but instead, he had complications. An infection kept him unable to play, unable even to practice.

Pittsburgh had to start its next season without Mario. He missed the first 50 games and only managed to play in 26 games all year.

But in 1991, the Penguins had a team that played well even without him. When he came back after missing those first 50 games, he was suddenly surrounded by real hockey players who could do more than fill in the rest of the Pittsburgh Penguins' team picture. With teammates like Paul Coffey, Kevin Stevens, Mark Recchi, Ron Francis, Jaromir Jagr, and Ulf Samuelsson, it was no longer easy for opponents to concentrate on Lemieux alone. It showed.

When Lemieux recovered his health, he was brilliant again. The Penguins stormed from behind the New York Rangers to capture the division title and head into the playoffs on a roll.

A major contributor was goalie Tom Barrasso. Barrasso had already won the Vezina Trophy as the best goalie in the league when he played for the Buffalo Sabres. The Penguins acquired Barrasso in 1988 when was only 23, and Pittsburgh figured that they were getting a key piece to what they hoped was a championship run.

As always with the Penguins, the story was Lemieux.

In the middle of the playoffs, things were shaky for a bit. The Boston Bruins actually led the Wales Conference finals two games to zero before the Penguins put their game in gear and swept the next four games to advance to the Stanley Cup finals.

Their opponents were the upstart Minnesota North Stars, who hadn't been expected to go anywhere in the playoffs but suddenly had a chance to land the vaunted Cup. The North Stars were a classic overachieving team that boasted no superstars but had a cohesion of play that stymied opponents with better-known players from more storied franchises.

In Game 1 in Pittsburgh, the North Stars were scrappy and resourceful and won 5-4. Despite Lemieux's breakaway in the second period—which occurred even though the Penguins had one fewer player because of a penalty—the North Stars refused to be intimidated. In the third period, the North Stars had a two-goal lead, but Lemieux almost managed to bring the Penguins back.

With 40 seconds left, Lemieux had a chance to tie the score but missed by mere inches. "I was counting the seconds," said a relieved Minnesota coach Bob Gainey,

Lemieux follows his opponents' moves closely while sitting on the bench.

"and Lemieux probably was too." Gainey added, "We put everything we had into this first game, as though it were the seventh."

But it was only Game 1. There was plenty of hockey left to play.

Game 2 featured one of Lemieux's most spectacular goals (see Chapter 1), and the Penguins went on to win 4-1 and tie the series at one game for each team.

Fifteen minutes prior to Game 3, as Lemieux was unlacing his skates after warmups, he had back spasms. He couldn't play.

Five minutes before the game, the North Stars received word that Lemieux was out. "It was like Christmas morning," said Minnesota winger Stew Gavin.

The North Stars won Game 3 by a score of 3–1. The winning goal was scored by North Stars center Bobby Smith, who would have been guarded by Lemieux had Lemieux been able to play.

The day after the game he missed, Lemieux said that he was starting to feel better. Sometimes, it just takes a day or so of rest, he explained. "When the spasms flare up," said Lemieux, "the more you do, the worse it gets."

By Game 4, whispers were beginning that the underdog North Stars just might be able to pull off a miracle. Of course, the miracle depended on Lemieux's bad back remaining bad. It didn't. When Super Mario warmed up for Game 4, he felt fine, and the North Stars knew that they wouldn't.

Lemieux's presence was not only felt as a physical factor but seemed to be psychological as well. In the first 2 minutes and 58 seconds of the game, the Penguins scored three goals. Two were scored while Lemieux was taking a break. The other goal was scored by Lemieux as Mark Recchi set him up right at the mouth of the goal. In the game, Lemieux battled as if his back had never bothered him. It was a physical game, and Lemieux was very physical as he chased down many loose pucks. The Penguins cruised to a 5-3 lead to tie the series at two games apiece. Jim Johnson of the North Stars said, "When Lemieux comes back, that team lifts off the ice."

In Game 5, Lemieux took over again. Early in the game, he scored during a penalty situation. For a minute and 58 seconds, the Penguins couldn't make use of their man advantage while a Minnesota player waited in the penalty box. But Lemieux put the puck home just two seconds before the North Stars had all of their players back on the ice. Lemieux's goal set the tone, and the Penguins took off from there to a 4-0 lead. The North Stars fought back valiantly, but the Penguins went on to win by a score of 6-4.

With one game left to win, the Penguins were on a roll. Having played in only four of the five games up to that point, Lemieux had already scored four goals, and he had an additional five assists.

In Game 6, the impossible dream of the North Stars became a nightmare. The Penguins scored early and often.

The best goal of the night was scored, once again, by Mario Lemieux. The Penguins were leading 1-0, but Minnesota had a power play. Nevertheless, Lemieux took off down the ice with the puck, made three sensational backhand to forehand moves, and then scored. The rampage was on, and the Penguins went on to win 8-0.

When it was over, Lemieux lifted the Stanley Cup and carried it for a victory lap around the Met Center.

"It was no strain on my back to lift it," he said.

He also won the Conn Smythe Trophy as the best player in the tournament.

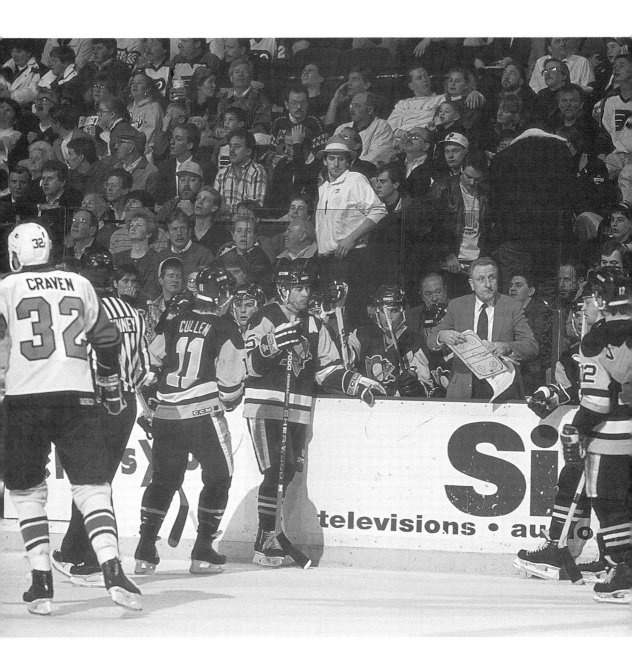

STANLEY CUP 2

The euphoria didn't last. Only 90 days after winning the Cup, the beloved coach of the Penguins, Bob Johnson, was diagnosed with brain cancer. It was swift and devastating. Johnson died on November 26, 1991.

The sadness was accompanied by turmoil. While Johnson was still fighting his illness, the team had hired an interim coach, Scotty Bowman. Bowman had been a coach and front office person for several hockey teams, but he inherited a club facing numerous problems.

The Penguins tried to adjust to a new coach while watching their Stanley Cup coach die. Johnson, who had only been with the team one year, had a grandfatherly demeanor that mixed perfectly with the Penguins. He was always positive and inspirational.

In addition, the Penguins were put up for sale. When the deal was finished, the new owners needed money, so they traded two of their

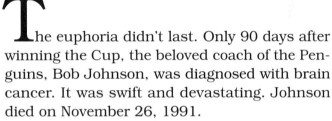

Coach Bob Johnson gathers the Penguins around him in a pregame meeting.

highest-paid players, Paul Coffey and Mark Recchi.

Because of all this, the Penguins had a lackluster regular season, finishing behind the New York Rangers. In the first round of the playoffs, the Washington Capitals jumped to a three games to one lead. The Penguins rallied to win in seven.

Next up were the New York Rangers, who had finished in first place. The Rangers jumped to a two games to one lead. In the first period of the second game, Ranger Adam Graves slashed his stick across Lemieux's left hand. Lemieux's hand was broken.

Graves later apologized, but many people felt that his hit was a deliberate attempt to deprive the Penguins of their best player. Deliberate or not, the hit had that effect. Pittsburgh had to play the remainder of that series without Lemieux. It showed how far the team had come since the early days of his career. Even without Lemieux, the Penguins won the next three straight against the Rangers.

Without Lemieux, the Penguins won the next game against the Boston Bruins in the next round. Then Lemieux came back, and they completed the sweep. In the final game against the Bruins, Lemieux scored two goals.

The opponents in the Stanley Cup finals were the Chicago Blackhawks. Going into the series, the Penguins had won seven games in a row. The Blackhawks had won 11.

The Blackhawks, though not a team loaded with superstars like Pittsburgh, were a gritty defensive-minded team with a couple of sharpshooters, Jeremy Roenick and Steve Larmer. They were also a rough-and-tumble team noted for their aggressive play. They came to challenge the Penguins to a game of physical hockey.

Lemieux lies on the ice after being injured in the second game against the Rangers in the 1992 playoffs.

Although Pittsburgh was favored, not many predicted a cakewalk. Game 1 started out as anything but a cakewalk. Chicago jumped out to a 3-0 lead in the first period.

Pittsburgh scored and then Chicago scored, and the Blackhawks led again by three goals. Late in the second period Rick Tocchet, acquired in the Coffey trade, and Lemieux both scored.

By late in the third period, Chicago still held a 4-3 lead. Then Jaromir Jagr, the 20-year-old phenom who was the perfect complement to Lemieux on the ice, took the puck and scored what Lemieux later called "the greatest goal I have ever seen."

Jagr's goal was stylish and difficult as he weaved the length of the ice through five Chicago defenders and then placed a low backhanded shot in the perfect spot past Chicago goalie Ed Belfour.

The score was tied. With 18 seconds left, Lemieux was on a breakaway when Steven Smith of Chicago tried to stop him by hooking his stick around Lemieux. Smith was called for a penalty. Pittsburgh was in a power play. Five seconds later, Lemieux scored.

Chicago coach Mike Keenan later accused Lemieux of faking his fall that led to the power play. "I can't respect Mario for diving," said Keenan. "The best player in the game is embar-

Ed Belfour leaps, but Lemieux is deadly when he has an open net in front of him. This goal came with 13 seconds left in Game 1 of the 1992 Stanley Cup finals. The Penguins won 5-4.

rassing himself and embarrassing the game."

Lemieux, who has been known to look for a sympathetic whistle from time to time, said, "I actually didn't dive that time."

Rather than get drawn into a war of words with Keenan, Lemieux let his play do the talking.

In Game 2, Lemieux scored two goals and the team went on to a 3-1 victory.

In that game, the Blackhawks tried a new strategy. Rather than try to outskate the Penguins with their scorers, they decided to try to be tougher. Pittsburgh forward Rick Tocchet told *Sports Illustrated*, "We're just as big and strong as they are, and it's not the worst thing to take a hit."

Despite his having already won a Stanley Cup championship, many scoring titles, and the Conn Smythe Trophy for the best player in the Stanley Cup Tournament in 1991, the questions about Lemieux continued.

The whispers were that he wasn't tough. That he would take a fall. That he didn't always try his hardest.

Former NHL goaltender John Davidson told *Sports Illustrated*, "One of the many things that Mario does well is conserve energy. He conserves fuel. People think he's lazy, but that's not true. He's just smart."

As for the goals he had scored, Lemieux was typically understated. "I'm playing some pretty good hockey right now," he said.

In Game 3, Kevin Stevens scored in the first period for Pittsburgh, and that was it. The game ended 1-0. The game displayed the hockey logic of starting a fight. In the last minute of the game, the Blackhawks had pulled out their goalie. The reason was to give Chicago one extra offensive player to score the tying goal. It was a desperation move.

Even more desperate was Chicago's Chris Chelios, who some said was goaded into a fight by Penguin Larry Murphy. "I saw them intercept a pass, and I figured the only way to stop them from getting an empty netter was to start an altercation. That's my excuse," said Chelios.

Chelios received a penalty, and the man advantage of pulling the goalie was gone. The fighting strategy didn't help and neither did anything else. The Penguins were clearly better than the Blackhawks.

The Blackhawks deserve some credit, though, because Game 4 offered some of the most exciting Stanley Cup finals hockey that has ever been played.

Blackhawk captain Dirk Graham especially excelled. Every time the Penguins scored in the first period, Graham followed it with a score. The Penguins scored three first-period goals, and Graham matched it with a first-period hat trick. A hat trick is when three goals are scored by one player in one game. Graham did it in a period.

At one point, the clubs scored three goals in 30 seconds. It was the fastest pace of scoring in the history of the Stanley Cup finals.

It was exciting, but in the end one team had Mario Lemieux and a three-game lead, and one didn't.

The final two goals of Game 4 were scored by Penguins Larry Murphy and Ron Francis. Lemieux had a goal and two assists. He ended up with 34 points for the playoffs.

Afterwards, no one was talking about whether Lemieux took a dive, but Lemieux, who had never commented on Keenan's attack, said sarcastically, "I'm going to go in the room and I'm going to dive into the Cup."

For the second year in a row, Lemieux won the Conn Smythe Trophy for being the best player in the tournament.

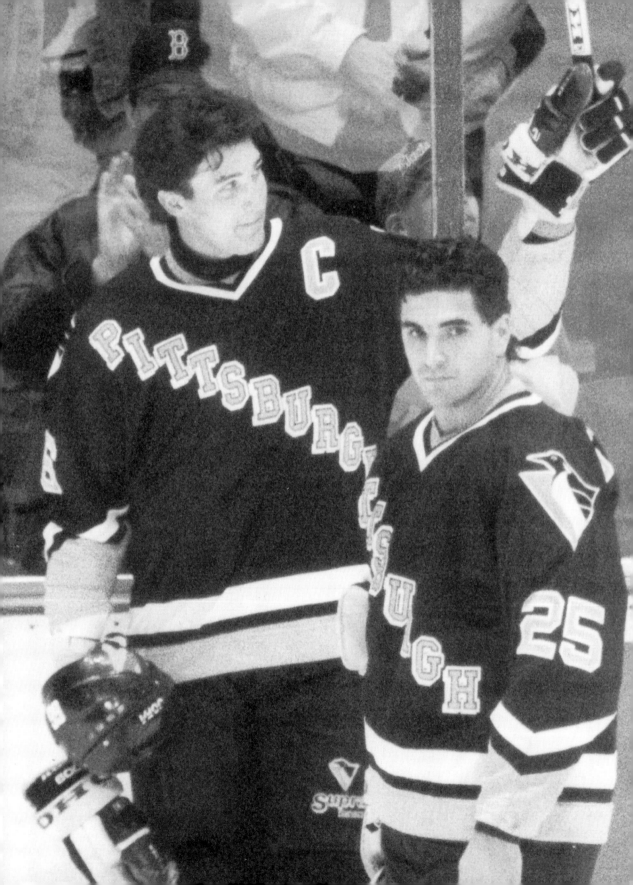

THE HAND OF FATE, HODGKIN'S DISEASE

Lemieux was known for his accomplishments and for his bad back. His personality? Well, he never gave much of a hint of himself to the public. He was quiet and reserved. He was not a showy athlete like so many who now star in shoe commercials and such. He was simply Mario.

His accomplishments were many. He had Stanley Cups and numerous scoring titles. After the Penguins won the second cup, he was given a new $42 million contract.

His bad back became a fact of life. Sometimes it acted up, sometimes it didn't. The surgery he had, which led to a subsequent infection, seemed to have helped some, but he still had spasms. When he did, he had to sit out.

On a cold Monday in January 1993, something happened to make the back problem, which had caused him to miss 103 games over the pre-

Lemieux acknowledges the standing ovation given him when he returned after receiving radiation treatments for Hodgkin's disease.

vious three and a half seasons, seem minor. Suddenly, even hockey was unimportant. Lemieux was diagnosed with Hodgkin's disease, a form of cancer.

Hodgkin's disease is characterized by the progressive enlargement of the lymph nodes and inflammation of some organs, such as the spleen and liver. It is named for the English physician who discovered it.

Cancer. Everyone in Pittsburgh remembered beloved coach Bob Johnson, who led the team to its first Stanley Cup and then died of a brain tumor in the same year.

"Any time you hear the word cancer, it's a scary thing," Lemieux said four days after his diagnosis. "When the doctors gave me the news, I could hardly drive home because of the tears, and I was crying the whole day. That certainly was the toughest day of my life."

He was already coming to a positive attitude by the time he met the media. "The more I found out about the disease, the better I've felt, and I've been great the last three or four days," he said.

Lemieux's Hodgkin's diagnosis came a year after he first noticed a small lump on his neck. At the time, Lemieux disregarded it, but six months later, he noticed that it had started to grow.

Finally, Lemieux brought the matter to the team's physician, Dr. Charles Burke, about two weeks prior to his diagnosis. "Mario was evaluated by our ear, nose, and throat consultant, Dr. Steve Jones, on January 5," said Burke. That night, Lemieux had back problems and played only one period.

Tests were recommended, and a CAT scan revealed an enlarged mass on his neck. The mass was removed and tested, and it was revealed to be Hodgkin's disease. However, Dr. Burke said, there was no evidence of it anywhere else in his body. Lemieux announced that he would undergo a month of radiation treatments.

Although hearing the news was a shock, Lemieux was typically thoughtful of others. The toughest part, he said, was telling his teammates. "I walked in Wednesday and everyone went silent," he said at that first press conference. "Kevin Stevens is always talking and Ulf Samuelsson is always yapping. It was tough for everybody and I wasn't sure what to say, and nobody else knew what to say." Lemieux added, "I've had the same experience, talking to people with cancer and not knowing what to say except good luck."

Lemieux was enjoying arguably his best and most injury-free year in quite a while. He was on a pace to threaten Wayne Gretzky's all-time single-season scoring record. He hadn't played close to a full season since 1988-89, when he played in 76 games.

Now the back pain really did seem minor. Even though all the doctors were very optimistic, no one was sure what to think.

The doctors tried to reassure. The kind of cancer Lemieux had is cured 90 percent of the time, they said. It would require radiation treatments of five minutes. Many of them—22 in all.

Despite the possibility of physical drain from radiation treatments, doctors were confident that Lemieux could return quickly to playing. "Dealing with issues of his hockey career and his return to play, we feel once treatment is completed he should be able to resume his career without interruption," said Dr. Burke. "I do not feel this will

Even after being sick and injured, Lemieux was still able to perform at the highest levels.

affect his long-term health, and it's certainly not life—or career—threatening."

So Lemieux took that dose of confidence, and he proceeded to use the power of his will in concert with the precision of the radiation treatments. He had his last radiation treatment on March 22, 1993. Afterward, he flew to Philadelphia.

That night, wearing a turtleneck to cover the areas left tender by the radiation treatment, he played his first game in two months.

When he came on the ice that night, the crowd, as was expected, stood and cheered. What wasn't expected, but probably should have been, was that the rough-and-tumble Philadelphia fans stood for more than a minute and cheered for a player from Pittsburgh.

Lemieux was moved. He appeared near tears. He waved his stick at the sellout crowd of 17,380 at the Spectrum.

Later, he scored a goal and had an assist, but the Philadelphia Flyers on went to win 5-4. "Anytime you have a serious injury or cancer, I think you have to have a lot of courage," Lemieux said that night. "If you don't, you aren't going to win the battle."

He added, "It's in my nature to fight back."

"I certainly missed the game," he commented, "but my main objective was to get back to 100 percent, and the game came second." He smiled. "Now, pretty much, the game is back on top again."

By the end of the season, he regained the scoring lead and won the scoring crown and league MVP. He had played only 60 games.

Lemieux's agent, attorney Tom Reich, said, "Mario has had an extraordinary season that has left us dumbfounded. I have made my living with words my whole career, but I have run out of words to describe Mario Lemieux. He is one heroic figure.

"It's obscene to be able to play at that level after such a long layoff," Reich continued. "But he's been just an unbelievable wellspring of strength."

Lemieux described his resiliency this way: "I didn't think about my cancer on a day-to-day basis. That certainly helped me get through it. I've been very positive since the beginning. I think that's my nature. Anytime you have some adversity, you must have courage."

Reich said that he was changed by his client's comeback. "He has created a light in my eye again that wasn't there when he was incapacitated. I said if he got back on the ice, I would never complain about anything again. He did— and I won't."

THE HEART
OF LEMIEUX

By the end of the remarkable 1993-94 season, Lemieux was exhausted. The effects of the radiation treatments had taken their toll. Despite the scoring title, Lemieux was out of gas. In the summer of 1994, word started getting out that Lemieux might retire or at least take a year off.

He fueled the talk in April by complaining about the style of play and quality of officiating in the league. He said that he might retire. It was an out-of-character blast and Lemieux caught some flak for it.

Boston Globe sportswriter Kevin Paul Dupont called his complaints "drivel, plain and simple nonsense from one more spoiled professional athlete who believes he is bigger than the game that has made him filthy rich and, in the process, turned him into a spoiled, petulant brat."

Many people said many things. Still, Lemieux had overcome cancer. He had a chronic bad back, and now he had anemia. In the spring, coming

Bill Lindsay of the Florida Panthers mugs Lemieux during their 1996 playoff game.

off a playoff loss, Lemieux was angry about the officiating.

Upon reflection in the summer, Lemieux was simply tired. He had been suffering anemia as a result of his radiation treatments for Hodgkin's disease.

So he announced that he was taking the 1994-95 year off. It was not an idle threat. It was a necessity for his health.

So he took a year off. It was not unprecedented. In fact, as hockey's biggest superstar took a year off, basketball's biggest superstar, Michael Jordan, was playing minor league baseball. Besides, Lemieux had plenty of reason to want time off.

It worked.

In June 1995, Lemieux announced to a ballroom packed with reporters that he would return for the 1995-96 season.

"I feel 100 percent better than I did last year," he said. "I have recuperated from the radiation treatments 100 percent and I also feel like my back has made tremendous progress over the last six months." The plan, said Lemieux, was for him to return for 60 or 70 games.

When he came back, he was as good as ever. That was quite good. In his first game, he had four assists. He was so good, in fact, that people liked to tell stories about his amazing accomplishments.

Boston Bruins president Harry Sinden told this story. "The Penguins were on the power play and I was watching from the press box. He had the puck, and I tell you in all honesty that at one point before he gave it up, every Bruin was lying on the ice. He had either faked or deceived them to the point where they all went down trying to stop his play, including our goalie. But they didn't score because the guy he passed it to missed an open net."

Lemieux's play inspired awe.

"There's a tendency to be afraid to make a move for fear that he'll make a fool of you," said Sinden. "When [retired Boston star] Bobby Orr played, he'd just blow by you. You didn't have a chance to make a fool of yourself, he was just gone. With Mario, he sometimes is standing still and people are falling down."

Two days after Sinden made his comments, Lemieux came to Boston and scored four goals. He received a standing ovation from the Boston crowd. "They don't do that for opposing players," said Penguins coach Eddie Johnston, who knows a bit about Boston crowds. Johnston had spent years as a Boston goaltender. The ovation "just tells you that they acknowledged the best player in the game today."

In February, Lemieux produced yet another spectacular goal that left many wide-eyed in astonishment. He was attacking Vancouver Canucks goalie Kirk McLean when the puck was knocked loose. Lemieux reached back between his legs and flipped the puck over McLean's shoulder into the top corner of the net. "He's so creative with the puck and something like that catches you off guard," said McLean. "You don't mind being on the highlight film when it's a guy like him."

Of course, there are no other guys like Lemieux.

"If you have a second chance to do something, you love it more," said Lemieux. "Sometimes you take it for granted, but when you miss it for a year and are able to come back, you feel different."

Lemieux immersed himself again in the world of hockey. He also found that he had an ability to inspire others with cancer, and he quickly went about that task as well.

"If people need help, if someone wants me to talk to a sick kid or a sick family member, it's something I want to do, something I feel I have a responsibility to do," said Lemieux. "I think, because of what I've been through, I'm a good example for people who need encouragement. I was able to come back and live a normal life."

He kept it mostly to himself. He didn't visit hospitals and sick children for publicity. He didn't do it because it would make him look good in the eyes of the fans, or in the eyes of reporters. He did it because he knew what it was like to have a terrible disease.

Although he had gone and visited hospitals before he became sick, he found that after his disease was diagnosed he had more to give. He was no longer just Mario Lemieux, the superstar hockey player. He was a cancer survivor. That meant a lot to those he

Mario's mom watches proudly as Lemieux accepts the Ross and Hart trophies.

visited. His message was: "You're going to be fine. If I can do it, you can too."

Lemieux met with kids from across the country. "We just talk about what the kids are going through," he told a journalist. "They want to talk to me about what I went through and what I did to come back. Not just to play, but to live a normal life. I do whatever I can to encourage them. The kids are inspiring to me."

One 15-year-old boy who was suffering from systemic lupus, an autoimmune deficiency disease, said that Lemieux's visit helped. "He made me feel normal. It was the best day of my life."

As for hockey, the comeback was, of course, a success. He led the Penguins to the best record in the tough Eastern Conference, and he won another scoring title.

Gretzky recognized Lemieux's remarkable achievement. "I think this season has been his best performance, and not just because he's coming back. The game is better now than it was four or five years ago. The players play a more defensive style now. The goaltending is better. His performance in that style of hockey is amazing."

Pittsburgh general manager Craig Patrick did not expect Lemieux to come back and be so dominant so quickly, but he wasn't surprised either. "I guess I'm semi-surprised, but we've become accustomed to Mario amazing us all the time. Every day is a new adventure with him. You sort of come to expect he's going to do something special today that he didn't do yesterday. But it is amazing what he's able to accomplish."

He has always done it in such an unassuming way. When he was once asked how he gets in shape for the season, he answered, "A month before the season, I stop putting ketchup on my french fries."

At the end of the 1995-96 season, there was speculation that Lemieux might call it a career. What more, after all, was there for him to accomplish? He had won five scoring titles and two Stanley Cups. He had cemented his place alongside Gretzky as one of the best players ever to lace up skates.

Besides, there were still all the lingering health problems. The bad back had not gone away. Sure, at times he was able to play through it, but at other times just lacing up skates caused a twinge that put him on the bench.

There were a million reasons to say goodbye and walk quietly into the sunset, but shortly before the 1996-97 season, Lemieux announced that he was coming back for one more season.

Why?

Simple.

He wanted to win the Stanley Cup again.

The message was clear. This comeback was not about scoring

Lemieux retired in 1997 and is a sure bet to make the Hall of Fame.

titles. It was not about proving that he could come back from health problems. As for those two reasons, well, he had been there, and done that.

This was simply about trying to win one more championship.

The Penguins had a fine season and Mario had an excellent one in 1996-97. For the fifth time in his career, Lemieux led the league in scoring. But the Penguins were ousted from the playoffs by the Philadelphia Flyers in the first round. (Philadelphia would go on to lose to the Detroit Red Wings in the Stanley Cup finals.) True to his word, Mario retired as soon as his team was eliminated. In a locker room interview, he pointed out that he had been playing hockey for all of his adult life. "I'm looking forward to trying something else," he said.

One of his new avocations will likely be golf. One other thing sure to get his attention: his family. His wife was pregnant with their fourth child at the time of his retirement.

Praise for Mario came from fans, teammates, and opponents. He had played in eight All-Star Games, and while he had played fewer years than his fans would have liked, there was no doubt that he had posted more highlights in his career than almost any other player.

"I've played with a lot of great players," said Paul Coffey, who as an Edmonton Oiler was once a teammate of Wayne Gretzky's. "Lemieux is definitely the most talented player I've played with."

Mario's career statistics are memorable. He finished first in goals per game, and second in assists per game and points per game; and he tied for second in career hat tricks. Plus he led the Penguins to two Stanley Cup championships.

Mario's prowess wasn't about getting endorsements. And unlike many athletes, he didn't really need a nickname.

His own last name is nickname enough: in French, Lemieux means simply "the best."

STATISTICS

MARIO LEMIEUX

Season	Team	Games	Goals	Assists	Points
1984-85	Pitt	73	43	57	100
1985-86	Pitt	79	48	93	141
1986-87	Pitt	63	54	54	108
1987-88	Pitt	77	70	98	168
1988-89	Pitt	76	85	114	199
1989-90	Pitt	59	45	78	123
1990-91	Pitt	26	19	26	45
1991-92	Pitt	64	44	87	131
1992-93	Pitt	60	69	91	160
1993-94	Pitt	22	17	20	37
1994-95	Pitt	0	0	0	0
1995-96	Pitt	70	69	92	161
1996-97	Pitt	76	50	72	122
Totals		745	613	882	1495

MARIO LEMIEUX
A CHRONOLOGY

1965 Born on October 5.

1981 Joins Laval Voisons.

1984 Scores 133 goals and 149 assists for Laval; picked number one in the draft by the Pittsburgh Penguins.

1985 Named NHL Rookie of the Year.

1986 Wins MVP award at the All-Star game.

1987 Teams with Wayne Gretzky on Canada Cup Team.

1988 Wins NHL scoring championship, Hart Trophy as NHL MVP, and the Lester Pearson Award.

1990 Undergoes back surgery.

1991 Helps lead Penguins to the first Stanley Cup championship.

1992 Leads Penguins to consecutive championships.

1993 Diagnosed with and treated for Hodgkin's Disease.

1996 After taking a season off, returns to hockey and wins scoring title.

1997 Retires; elected into the Hockey Hall of Fame.

1999 Buys the Pittsburgh Penguins, increasing ticket sales and bringing the franchise back from bankruptcy.

SUGGESTIONS FOR FURTHER READING

Gutman, Bill, *Mario Lemieux: Wizard With a Puck*. Brookfield, CT: Millbrook Press, 1992.

Scher, John, "I'll Be Back When I'm Cured." *Sports Illustrated*, January 25, 1993.

Scher, John, "Netminder's Nightmare." *Sports Illustrated*, November 16, 1992.

ABOUT THE AUTHOR

Brian Tarcy is a freelance writer who lives on Cape Cod, Massachusetts.

PICTURE CREDITS: Bruce Bennett Studios: 2, 28, 31, 35, 50, 56, 58; Michael DiGirolamo/Bruce Bennett Studios: 6, 38; Reuters/Corbis-Bettmann: 8, 42, 47; UPI/Corbis-Bettmann: 20, 25; AP/Wide World Photos: 22, 32, 41, 52.

INDEX